D1057944

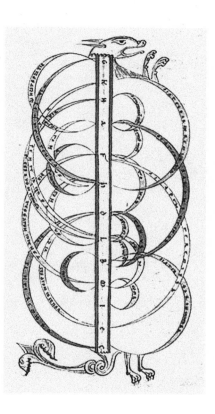

Published by
Walker Publishing Company, Inc., New York

Printed on recycled paper.

Library of Congress Cataloging-in-Publication Data
has been applied for.

ISBN-10: 0-8027-1682-2
ISBN-13: 978-0-8027-1682-8

Visit Walker & Company's Web site
at www.walkerbooks.com

First U.S. edition 2008

3 5 7 9 10 8 6 4 2

Designed and typeset by
Wooden Books Ltd, Glastonbury, UK

Printed in the United States of America

THE ELEMENTS OF
MUSIC

MELODY, RHYTHM, & HARMONY

Jason Martineau

Walker & Company
New York

for someone special

With gratitude to my mother and father for their support in my life pursuits. Also thanks to: John Martineau, Gary DeSorbo, Dr. Bruce Bennett, Dr. David Conte, Peter O'Hanrahan, David Saÿen, Alan Tower, Marcus Shelby, and the many composers, performers, artists, and thinkers that have inspired me over the years. Thanks to the Alexander Turnbull Library for permission to reproduce the Boethius frontispiece.

Above: The Lute Player and the Harpist, *Israhel van Meckenem, c. 1500.*
Title page: The Musical Society, *Abraham Bosse, 1635.*
Frontispiece: Zoomorphic musical diagram, from Boethius De Musica, *480-524.*

CONTENTS

Introduction	1
What Is Music?	2
Epigrams and Dialectics	4
Acoustics and Overtones	6
Understanding Scales	8
Meet the Intervals	10
Basic Rhythms	12
Tone Tendencies	14
Basic Harmonies	16
Basic Melody	18
Chord Progressions	20
Instrumentation	22
More Complex Rhythms	24
Form and Structure	26
More Complex Harmonies	28
Tonality and Modulation	30
Modal, Tonal, Dronal	32
The Three Minors	34
More Intervals	36
Further Melodic Elements	38
Complex Chord Progressions	40
Around the World	42
Advanced Harmonies	44
Advanced Forms	46
Putting It All Together	48
Glossary of Terms	50
Appendix I – Basic Notation	52
Appendix II – Scales	54
Appendix III – Selected Rhythms	56
Appendix IV – Harmonies	57
Appendix V – Solfege and Mnemonics	58

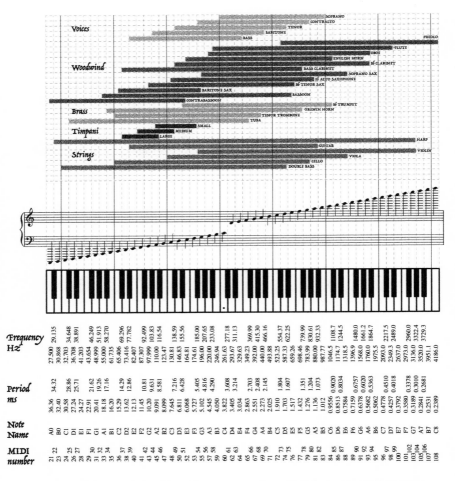

Above: Just over seven octaves of the audible spectrum, centered on middle C, showing the positioning of different instruments within the range of audible frequencies. Data for frequency and period is given for equal temperament.

INTRODUCTION

Music is the art medium that communicates interiority, being only perceived by the ears, and received by the mind. A strict approach to understanding music will consequently always have something lacking as music theory, in essence, is primarily descriptive and not prescriptive. The tendencies and practices in music are only observed and cataloged upon analysis, after the fact. It is the hearts and minds of human beings that shape and weave melodies, harmonies, and rhythms together into meaningful tapestries, imbued with the interior landscapes of their immediate experiences.

Much of the theory in this book is based upon the European classical tradition, starting around the early 18th century. The content is designed to get you started in understanding the relationships of the tones and rhythms, and in unpacking the inherent properties of sound in the process, and then, perhaps, music in general.

For the purposes of this book all principles are presented assuming equal temperament, the prevalent tuning system for over 300 years. The word "tone" and "note" may sometimes be used interchangeably, but generally "tone" refers to the audible sound, and "note" refers to the written symbol. Other terms can be consulted in the glossary. The deeper mathematics behind temperament and the tuning of scales are covered in *Harmonograph*, by Anthony Ashton.

I hope this book will reveal how the underlying harmonic template of sound acts as an organizational framework from which the fabric of music is woven, influencing our perception of accord, discord, tension and release, telling a story, making a journey.

WHAT IS MUSIC?
and all that jazz

Music is ... a mother's lullaby. It gives sound to our feelings when we have no voice, words when we are silent. In it we praise, love, hope, and remember. The breath of the soul, the contours of the path of a hummingbird in flight, and the wind that carries it, music shapes and shivers into endless colors, nuanced and diverse, and eternally creative. It is Spirit taking form.

Music is carried by the vibrations of molecules of air, like waves upon an ocean. It perhaps uniquely captures and conveys the interior landscape of one human mind to another, holding our tears and sweat, pain and pleasure, packaged as paeans and preludes and etudes and nocturnes. It is the texturization of the deliquescence of time, the ebb and flow of mood and meaning. It ruminates, vacillates, contemplates, and stimulates.

In music we organize and fantasize, arranging the elements of music—*melody*, *rhythm*, and *harmony*—into meaningful shapes and patterns. Its rhythms move our hands, feet and bodies to the pulses of the universe. Its harmonies breathe with the exploratory intricacies and curiosities of relationship and proportion, consonance, dissonance, assonance, and resonance. Its melodies flitter into flights of fancy, weaving woe and wonder.

When music is married to language, then what is spoken becomes song, elevating the intentions and entreating us to listen more deeply, making the profane sacred. Music soothes the soul, and the savage beast. Orpheus mystifies creatures and trees, changing the course of rivers, outplaying the Sirens' song with his lyre. Radha and Krishna play the flute and dance jubilantly.

"Temple Of Music" by Robert Fludd (1574-1637). At lower left Pythagoras discovers that the ratios of hammer weights correspond to the octave, fifth, and fourth. On the wall lower right the basic rhythms are notated along a bass staff. Above these are the three kinds of hexachords, the six-note scales of medieval music. To the left of this is the lambda, a matrix of note relationships and ratios going back to Plato. The upper diagonal portion of that region is a diagram of intervallic distances between pitches in the scale. Running vertically further left is the monochord. Above the diagonal matrices is an actual composition putting all these practices into a musical structure.

EPIGRAMS AND DIALECTICS
ideas in sound

When music parallels language, it often chooses devices that resemble epigrams or poetic devices. Take the epigram "Live, Love, Learn." This collection of words, when arranged together, takes on an emergent inter-associative meaning that transcends the individual parts. Notice the alliteration of "L"s, and the use of "learn" in the sequence to diffuse the rhyming scheme of the first two words, and close the set. Additionally, all three words are monosyllabic, and can be used both as conceptual infinitives (to live, to love, to learn) and as imperatives (Live! Love! Learn!).

In both music and language the components of epigrams are often synthesized or unified through paradox, an essential quality for having an aesthetic response and remembering the phrase. In music notes rise and fall, are consonant and dissonant, *staccato* and *legato*, or push and pull one another, these fundamental dualities representing the paradoxical nature of reality itself. Small pieces of meaning are arranged from them into larger forms based on their structure, and, perceiving this unity of opposites, the listener is temporarily removed from the dualistic separated stream of everyday life into the realm of unification.

The "Happy Birthday" melody epigram (*see opposite*) undergoes various permutations and transformations but retains its fundamental characteristics, and thus stays satisfyingly recognizable to the end.

4

Above: "Happy Birthday". The melody starts on the 5th of the major scale, a long note followed by a short, repeated, then the 6th to the 5th, and a leap upwards of a fourth to the octave, before falling a half step. The first repetition of this idea is the same, except the leap upward is now larger (a fifth) followed by a fall of a whole step. The third time it is followed by a leap upwards of an entire octave (small interval becomes large), and where the melody previously fell by one step, now it falls twice, with a salient dissonance on the person's name elongated on a strong beat. The final phrase repeats the opening lyric, on a dissonant tone, falling by step, leaping down, and another step. A well-constructed dialectic of leaps and steps, up and down, resting and moving tones, alternating on strong and weak beats, carrying us effortlessly on a tiny journey, a slow striving ascent upward, and a gentle cascade downward, parachuting to the tonic or home key of the piece.

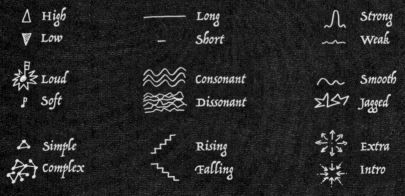

△ High	—— Long	∩ Strong
▽ Low	– Short	∼∼ Weak
Loud	≋ Consonant	∼ Smooth
♪ Soft	≋ Dissonant	⋝⋀⋝ Jagged
△ Simple	⌐⌐ Rising	Extra
Complex	⌐⌐ Falling	Intro

Above: Much of the communication of meaning in music is dependent upon opposites. Chromatic-diatonic, leap-step, repeat-contrast ... opposites interplay as the narrative unfolds to carry the listener along. Contexts are defined immediately by the first sounds the music presents, and all that follows is constantly compared to what precedes, in the short-term and long-term, as time passes. Thus the interplay of these dialectics becomes clear as the music unfolds. Opposites in conflict create drama; opposites in accord appear as beauty.

ACOUSTICS AND OVERTONES
from one note to seven and beyond

Any sound that can be perceived as a pitch or tone will have some periodicity in it, vibrating at a regular frequency with a specific mixture of *overtone* amplitudes (*see opposite*), creating a distinctive *timbre*. An oboe, sitar, or piano can all play the same tone, yet sound different. The vowels A, E, I, O, and U are created by the trapping or releasing of overtones with the shape of the mouth and lips.

The other component of sound, *noise*, has no periodicity—a hammer striking, a finger plucking, a bow scraping, the sound on a television with no signal. Bands of noise are named by color (white noise, pink noise, gray noise), and are part of the musical sounds an instrument can produce. The noise component of a sound can be compared to the consonants in language, with drums as *plosives*, shakers as *fricatives*, and cymbals as *sibilants*.

Essentially, musical sound can be described much in the way language sound can: a combination of tones that vary overtone content with a noise component that initiates the sound, sometimes continues it, and occasionally also closes it, the function of consonants, with an organizing rhythm and form.

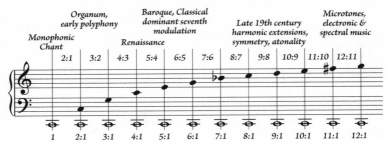

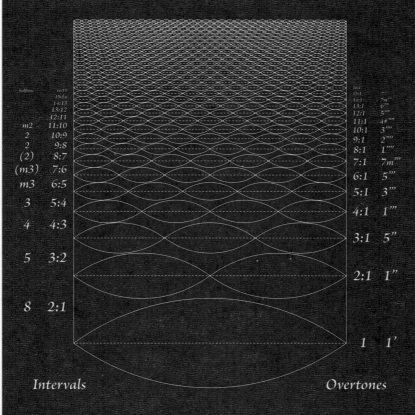

halftone			1c:1	
	16:15		15:1	7‴
	15:14		14:1	7m‴
	14:13		13:1	6‴
	13:12		12:1	5‴
	12:11		11:1	4#‴
m2	11:10		10:1	3‴
2	10:9		9:1	2‴
2	9:8		8:1	1‴
(2)	8:7		7:1	7m‴
(m3)	7:6		6:1	5‴
m3	6:5		5:1	3‴
3	5:4		4:1	1‴
4	4:3		3:1	5″
5	3:2		2:1	1″
8	2:1		1	1'

Intervals   *Overtones*

Above: As a string vibrates, or tube fills with air, proportional waveforms are created in whole-number ratios that occupy the same space, giving rise to the harmonic series or overtones. Unity subdivides into infinitely smaller units. Each one of these overtones is a station or stopping point, a gravitational pole acting upon other tones nearby.

Left: The history of music in the West can be seen as a parallel to the overtone series, ascending upward and incorporating more and more of the series into harmonic thought. The relative distances of the intervals also suggest the time spent exploring those intervals, a journey from iconic objectivity to interior complexity.

Understanding Scales
streets and stairways

A scale is a collection of discrete tones that are a subset of the pitch continuum and that normally climb an octave in a certain number of steps, often seven. Most of the unique and beautifully diverse musical scales from around the world owe a large part of their heritage to the overtone series and use the fifth, the first tuned note, as the fundamental unit. Fifths are piled up, one atop another, and then transposed back down to a single octave. Thirds can also be prioritized to derive a scale (e.g., meantone tuning) and a myriad of other methods all sculpt the different tuning systems that have emerged—each of them trying to solve the problem of locking a fluid, infinite curve or spiral into a grid or circle. The scale becomes a playground for a melodic drama unfolding the relative tensions of these overtones with the tones between them.

The basic stations are: 1–3–5–1, created by the overtones 2:1 (the octave, the only note that when reached gives the distinctive impression of the fundamental tone below it, the same, yet different), then from 3:1, the 5, which has the next quality of sameness, though it is in fact a different pitch entirely. Then 4:1, another octave, then 5:1, which becomes the 3, generally conveying the major or minor quality of a chord, scale, or melody. Many 5-note and 7-note scales utilize this underlying structure, and in many variations, but the fundamental structures are 1-2-3-5-6 and 1-2-3-4-5-6-7. Seven is born from five.

A 7-note scale in a 12-note environment means that 5 notes will always be missing. In Middle-Eastern systems 7 notes are chosen (in performance) from 17; in India 7 are chosen from 22.

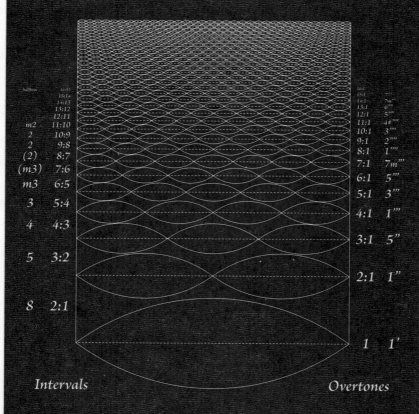

halftone			
	1e:15	16:1	
	15:14	15:1	7m""
	14:13	14:1	
	13:12	13:1	6""
	12:11	12:1	5""
m2	11:10	11:1	4#""
2	10:9	10:1	3""
2	9:8	9:1	2""
(2)	8:7	8:1	1""
(m3)	7:6	7:1	7m"'
m3	6:5	6:1	5"'
3	5:4	5:1	3"'
4	4:3	4:1	1"'
5	3:2	3:1	5"
		2:1	1"
8	2:1		
		1	1'

Intervals   *Overtones*

Above: As a string vibrates, or tube fills with air, proportional waveforms are created in whole-number ratios that occupy the same space, giving rise to the harmonic series or overtones. Unity subdivides into infinitely smaller units. Each one of these overtones is a station or stopping point, a gravitational pole acting upon other tones nearby.

Left: The history of music in the West can be seen as a parallel to the overtone series, ascending upward and incorporating more and more of the series into harmonic thought. The relative distances of the intervals also suggest the time spent exploring those intervals, a journey from iconic objectivity to interior complexity.

UNDERSTANDING SCALES
streets and stairways

A scale is a collection of discrete tones that are a subset of the pitch continuum and that normally climb an octave in a certain number of steps, often seven. Most of the unique and beautifully diverse musical scales from around the world owe a large part of their heritage to the overtone series and use the fifth, the first tuned note, as the fundamental unit. Fifths are piled up, one atop another, and then transposed back down to a single octave. Thirds can also be prioritized to derive a scale (e.g., meantone tuning) and a myriad of other methods all sculpt the different tuning systems that have emerged—each of them trying to solve the problem of locking a fluid, infinite curve or spiral into a grid or circle. The scale becomes a playground for a melodic drama unfolding the relative tensions of these overtones with the tones between them.

The basic stations are: 1–3–5–1, created by the overtones 2:1 (the octave, the only note that when reached gives the distinctive impression of the fundamental tone below it, the same, yet different), then from 3:1, the 5, which has the next quality of sameness, though it is in fact a different pitch entirely. Then 4:1, another octave, then 5:1, which becomes the 3, generally conveying the major or minor quality of a chord, scale, or melody. Many 5-note and 7-note scales utilize this underlying structure, and in many variations, but the fundamental structures are 1-2-3-5-6 and 1-2-3-4-5-6-7. Seven is born from five.

A 7-note scale in a 12-note environment means that 5 notes will always be missing. In Middle-Eastern systems 7 notes are chosen (in performance) from 17; in India 7 are chosen from 22.

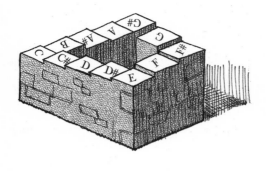

Left: This modified Penrose staircase shows the paradox of the musical octave. As we traverse a scale either ascending or descending, there is a simultaneous departure and return; we are coming and going at the same time.

Half steps: In chromatic tuning, e.g., on a keyboard, the distance from any note to its neighbor, white or black, is a half step or semitone. Western chromatic tuning has twelve equal half steps to the octave. C-C#-D-D#-E-F-F#-G-Ab-A-Bb-B-C

Whole steps: Whole steps or tones are equivalent to two half steps. They too can traverse white or black, depending upon where they fall on the keyboard. The pair of mutually exclusive scales made solely of whole steps are: C-D-E-F#-G#-Bb and Db-Eb-F-G-A-Cb

Half steps

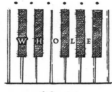

Whole steps

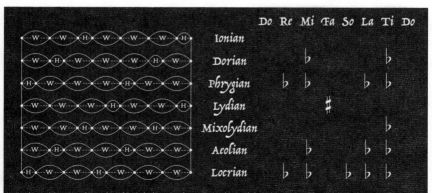

Above: The seven classical modes with their Greek names. Left: By sliding the starting point of the scale set one note to the right, all whole steps and half steps move to the left, creating six further modes from a seven note scale. Right: A way to generate the modes compared to the major scale (Ionian) by making a few chromatic adjustments, flat or sharp.

MEET THE INTERVALS
and the circle of fifths

A musical interval is the distance between two tones, and although tuned slightly differently from culture to culture, the same intervals are broadly found all over the world. Intervals can be thought of in two ways: The first is as an ever-contracting series of simple frequency ratios, so that the first interval (the *octave*) is a 2:1 relationship, the second (the *fifth*) is 3:2, and the third (the *fourth*) is 4:3. Then follow the *major third* of 5:4, the *minor third* of 6:5, the *second* of 9:8 or 10:9, and yet smaller intervals, with names like the *quarter tone*, *shruti*, *li*, *comma*, *apotome*, and *microtone*, depending upon the era and culture.

The second way of looking at this series is to compare intervals to the fundamental to which they all relate. This approach results in an octave (2:1), a fifth (3:1), another octave (4:1), a major third (5:1), another fifth (6:1), a seventh (7:1), another octave (8:1), a second (9:1), a third (10:1), and a *tritone* (11:1), etc. If the first view is relative, with each partial compared to its nearest neighbor, then the second view is absolute, as intervals take an absolute value compared to the fundamental. Both views are useful when taking an analytical approach to the construction of musical scales and the melodies that ultimately derive from them.

Notice the octave, fifth, and major third appearing in both systems. All scales around the world broadly contain these intervals in some form, with their precise tuning revealing slight variations and nuances in instrument construction and cultural tastes. Those using the first approach tune their instruments and derive their scales by the relationship of each overtone to one another, while others using the second approach relate intervals to their fundamental.

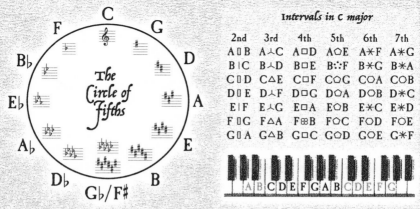

Intervals in C major

	2nd	3rd	4th	5th	6th	7th
	A▯B	A⅄C	A▢D	A◇E	A✳F	A✱G
	B∣C	B⅄D	B▢E	B∴F	B✳G	B✱A
	C▯D	C△E	C▢F	C◇G	C◇A	C◇B
	D∣E	D⅄F	D▢G	D◇A	D◇B	D✱C
	E∣F	E⅄G	E▢A	E◇B	E✳C	E✱D
	F▯G	F△A	F⊗B	F◇C	F◇D	F◇E
	G▯A	G△B	G▢C	G◇D	G◇E	G✱F

|A|B|C|D|E|F|G|A|B|C|D|E|F|G|

Above left: The circle of fifths is a diagram of common tones. Chromatic notes (sharps and flats) are added in the order of perfect fifths to preserve the whole and half step relationships in the major scale built upon any note. Any consecutive seven fifths on the circle yield all the notes in any one of the twelve major scales. Accidentals occur whenever an alteration to a scale must be made to preserve the syntax of the alphabet. Opposing notes on the wheel form a tritone, the symmetrical interval that cuts the octave in half.
Above right: A table of the intervals present in the key of C major, the white notes on a piano.

Right: A symbolic system of glyphs used in this book for describing musical intervals and their relative sizes. Note the shapes expanding and contracting with the size of the interval. Minor and diminished intervals are smaller by one semitone than their respective major and Perfect counterparts. Augmented intervals are one semitone larger than perfect. Major and minor are sometimes referred to as hard and soft (dur and moll).

The lower part of the diagram shows the symmetrical nature of the consonances of the intervals. Unison, the fourth, fifth and octave are perfect. Thirds and sixths are imperfect consonances, while seconds and sevenths are dissonances.

		2nd	3rd			6th	7th
(m)inor		∣	⅄			✳	✱
(M)ajor		▯	△			⬡	⬡
		1st		4th	5th		8ve
(d)iminished		∴		∴	∴		
(P)erfect	○			▢	⬠		∞
(A)ugmented				⊞	⬡		

Consonances

perfect
imperfect
dissonant
perfect

11

BASIC RHYTHMS
meter and the big beat

Rhythm is the component of music that punctuates time, carrying us from one beat to the next, and it subdivides into simple ratios just like pitch. Even in seemingly complex rhythms an underlying structure based on groupings of divisions into 2 and 3 is often perceptible. The march and the waltz are thus nodes in the subdivision of rhythm, and the tensions created by *polyrhythms* and *syncopation* push and pull against the gravity of these nodes, just as individual musical notes do in a scale. All of this happens through time, creating a framework of epigrams, disclosing their plight or journey, existing within a system of rules.

Rhythmic structures are organized into *measures* for the purpose of notation, which denote time parceled into groups of beats. In 4/4, each measure has four beats marked by quarter notes, which often show up in groups of four measures. Within most rhythms a pulse of strong and weak beats, or strong and weak parts of beats, also exists, and *chords* are placed in each measure at either the *anacrusis* or the *ictus*, "between" or "upon" the beats, to convey harmonic movement and reinforce the sense of tonality. The unfolding and varying of the resulting tensions and releases through time is responsible for much of the emotive and expressive power of rhythm.

The rate at which events pass is also a crucial component of any rhythmic texture, often measured by beats per minute (bpm). A pulse's subdivisions are partly meaningless without knowing its rate or *tempo*.

bpm: 40   *largo*   60   *adagio*   76   *andante*   108   *moderato*   120   *allegro*   168   *presto*   200

12

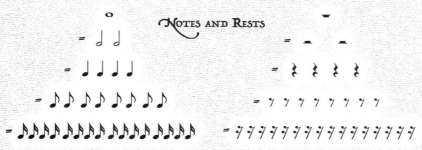

NOTES AND RESTS

Above: The basic duple subdivisions of the beat as notes (left) and rests (right). The values are, from top to bottom, whole, half, quarter, eighth, and sixteenth. This process can continue up to one-hundred-twenty-eighth notes. The rest occupies the same potential space as a note does, and provides breath and space, helping to clarify different parts.

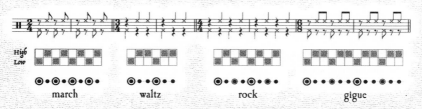

High
Low

march   waltz   rock   gigue

Musical styles are often expressed by their rhythmic patterns, and the grouping and subgrouping of their component strong and weak beats. Shown here are some of the most basic ones, built upon 2 and 3, simple and compound.

In a time signature, the numerator indicates the number of beats per measure, and the denominator indicates which subdivision will receive the beat. The measure, or bar, separated by lines, indicates a rhythmic cell, one repetition of the basic grouping or cycle.

LONG AND SHORT

Duples	Triples
Iamb $\vert$ —	Tribrach $\vert\vert\vert$
Trochee — $\vert$	Dactyl — $\vert\vert$
Spondee — —	Amphibrach $\vert$ — $\vert$
Dibrach $\vert\vert$	Anapest $\vert\vert$ —
	Bacchius $\vert$ — —
	Antibacchius — — $\vert$
	Amphimacer — $\vert$ —
	Molossus — — —

The poetic feet measure all the possible combinations of long and short in duple and triple groupings, twelve total.

TONE TENDENCIES
tension and release

Because of the powerful gravity and stability of the stations of the scale, notes that deviate from these are perceived as transitional. Whole and half steps, and even minor and major thirds, all manifest varying degrees of tension, which is then released when a station is reached, or when transitional notes are traded for less dynamic transitional notes. Additionally, notes that are farther from a stopping point or station are less active or dramatic in relation to it than adjacent ones. Minor scales have basically the same set of tensions as major scales (*see page 34*).

A further level of complexity occurs in music that has chord progressions and modulations, as the set of tensions can change. Here the initial root, third, and fifth of a chord (and scale) are the stations, with the rest of the tones intermediary, but as the chord changes, the root, third, and fifth of the new chord become the new stations, or secondary stations. However, without an actual modulation, the importance of the primary set of relations is not lost in memory, and a tiered set of relationships is created. Since chords can be constructed with any note of the scale as a root, they can both take on the same stable or transitional aspects as the roots upon which they are built already possess, and contain their own subset of stations, forming two tiers of stability or instability working at any given moment. The genius of a good melody involves the understanding of these two tiers of relationships, and the skillful implementation of manipulating expectation and result against those natural tensions, based largely upon the utilization of memory, incorporating expectation and fulfillment.

Western	**Do**	**Re**	**Mi**	**Fa**	**So**	**La**	**Ti**	**Do**
	ROOT	ROUSING	STEADY	DESOLATE	GRAND	SAD	LEADING TONE	
	FIRM	HOPEFUL	CALM	AWE	BRIGHT	WEEPING	PIERCING	
Indian	**Sa**	**Re**	**Ga**	**Ma**	**Pa**	**Da**	**Ni**	**Sa**
	BASIS	JOY	ANGER	CLEANSING	SPEECH	NIGHT	AGITATED	
	STRONG	SEXUALITY	WRATH	YIN	YANG	PLEASURE	EFFORT	

Above: The seven tones of the major scale, their Curwen hand signs, and associated qualities. Horizontal hand signs indicate the stations, the others signify the tendencies of the intermediary tones, pushing down or pulling up.

Above: The main theme of the 2nd movement of Beethoven's Pathétique Sonata in A♭ Major with Kodaly hand signs. The accidentals (E-natural in bar 5 and A-natural in bar 7) act as temporary leading tones, so they receive the "ti" hand.

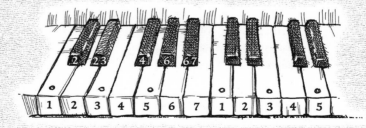

Above: Intermediary tones each come in varying flavors. The second can be either lowered, natural, or raised; the fourth can only be natural or raised. If it were lowered it would become the third. The sixth can come in three flavors, but the seventh is also limited, for it can only be lowered or natural. If it were to be raised it would become the octave.

BASIC HARMONIES
triangles and triads

The major triad, which occurs naturally in the harmonic series as a pair of thirds (a major, then a minor, adding to a fifth), is the foundation of tertial music (chords constructed in thirds) around the world, the perfect fifth and major third being, after the octave, the most stable and resonant intervals, derived from the overtones.

Moving a note from the bottom to the top of a triad creates an inversion (*below*), with the same notes, but with a new bass. Notice how major triads in first inversion have two minor intervals, giving them an opposite flavor. The same holds true of minor chords, which in their first inversion sound markedly major, since two of their three intervals are major. Diminished and augmented chords are often said to be rootless, as they have no stable fourth or fifth.

Inversions conspire to strengthen or weaken the importance of the root. In root position the fundamental intervals are all in place as in the overtone series, the bottom note receiving the identity of the chord built upon it. In the first inversion, the third of the chord is in the bass but has no strong intervals above it to emphasize its importance. Instead, the root, now at the top, is supported by a perfect fourth just below it, another strong architectural interval. The same is true with the fifth in the bass, the second inversion, where a perfect fourth again supports the root. The combined notes thus always point to their root position, stacked in thirds.

16

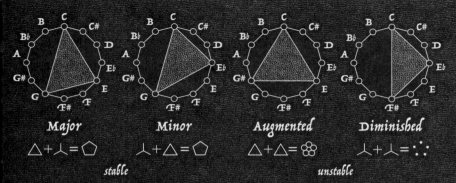

Major Minor Augmented Diminished

$\triangle + \curlywedge = \pentagon$ $\curlywedge + \triangle = \pentagon$ $\triangle + \triangle = \bigoplus$ $\curlywedge + \curlywedge = \therefore$

stable unstable

Above: The four chord qualities of triads, two stable, and two unstable. Symmetrical chords sound unresolved or unstable, while asymmetrical chords sound stable because of the presence of the perfect fifth, the only interval (with its inversion, the fourth) that does not divide the octave equally. Changing the fifth by one half step, in either case, produces symmetry and instability. Perfect fourths and fifths are the architecture of the system that contain the fluid symmetry of all the other intervals.

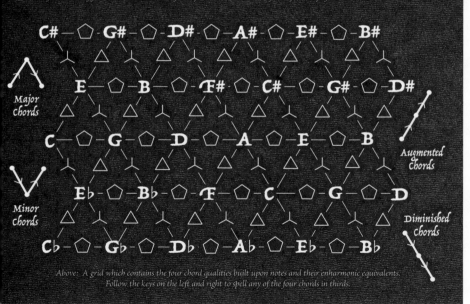

Above: A grid which contains the four chord qualities built upon notes and their enharmonic equivalents. Follow the keys on the left and right to spell any of the four chords in thirds.

17

BASIC MELODY
steps and leaps, contour and gesture

A melody is created by the succession of tones through time. Step by step, note by note, an outline is formed, a path carved. Gestures appear, like the inflections used in speech, or the dialectic of rising and falling tones, or the contrast of high and low notes. A distant leap feels large and grandiose, a small one more fluid and gentle. Curved or jagged contours can be suggested.

Melodies are normally a mixture of small *steps* and larger *leaps*, with a leap in one direction inducing a yearning for completion by a step in the opposite direction, leaving a gap to be filled in. The continuous nature of melody means that when notes stray far, the listener, following the path to find out where it leads, likes them to remain connected and return. This is often manifested by a rhythmic intertwining of tones in and out of the stations of the scale.

The expressivity of a melody comes in part by the tension and release of the intermediary notes of the scale, their rhythmic placement on a strong or weak beat intensifying or diminishing their effect. Sometimes a melody can act as two melodies, by leaping up and down, thus alternately maintaining two independent threads, each on their own pitch level (or *register*). Other melodies rely on pitches predominantly rising or falling for their effect.

Melodies in vocal music are either *melismatic*, with many pitches to one syllable, or *syllabic*, with one pitch per syllable.

Silent pauses, or rests (*caesura*) are essential to melodies. They allow time for breath, reflection, and interaction with the music. Listeners wait for the next event, suspended, anticipating. A well-placed rest in a theme can be a powerful musical moment.

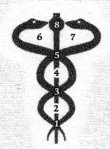

Above: Melodies are easily expressed visually. They weave between the strong stations of the scale and the weaker, transitional parts, which contribute to the tensionality and expressive shape of any melody.

Upper Neighbor
Decorates a station from above, weak beat

Lower Neighbor
Decorates a station from below, weak beat

Passing Tone
Acts as a bridge between two stations, weak beat

Appoggiatura
A non-station event that leans on a station, strong beat

Escape Tone (éschappée)
A non-station note that escapes a step in one direction and leaps in the other

Cambiata
A neighbor group, upper and lower, often dissonances decorating a station

Non-station notes can be either accented or unaccented, falling on strong or weak beats (except the appoggiatura, which is always accented). When they occur on strong beats, they compete more strongly with the stations to convey the harmony.

Trill   Trill   Mordent   Turn   Grace note

Above: Melodic ornaments and embellishments, such as (from left to right) trills, mordents, turns, and grace notes, are also melodic formulae, on the smallest scale.

CHORD PROGRESSIONS
tonic, dominant, and subdominant

Chords take on the identity of the station upon which they are built, reinforced by the tone tendencies, so that as the chords move in a progression or succession, they push and pull on their neighbors, reinforcing the key. As notes in a chord collaborate to emphasize one pitch, all chords collaborate to strengthen or weaken the tonic.

The strongest progressive motion a root can have is a fifth, either downward or upward, highlighting the close kinship and relative gravity of three consecutive pitches on the circle of fifths. The most basic chord movement then is *tonic* (I) to *subdominant* (IV) to *dominant* (V) and back to tonic (I), although other triads in the scale can substitute for these three basic functions without sacrificing wholly the function or temporal meaning of their placement (*below*). I and iii share 3 and 5, so can substitute for each other. Likewise, ii and IV share two tones, as do vi and I, and V and vii°. The more common tones, the smoother and more gradual the harmonic motion.

There are essentially three states in tonal harmonic progression: starting, departing, and returning, which are repeated and cycled to reinforce the tonic. Chords with more symmetrical intervals (thirds) are unstable or require resolving, and have a dominant function, while harmonies having perfect fourths and fifths (the only asymmetric intervals) are more restful and are non–dominant.

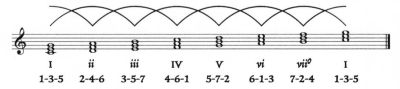

I	ii	iii	IV	V	vi	vii°	I
1-3-5	2-4-6	3-5-7	4-6-1	5-7-2	6-1-3	7-2-4	1-3-5

DOMINANT (active)	☀	5	V
MEDIANT	○	3	iii
SUPERTONIC	○	2	ii
TONIC (HOME)	🜨	1	I
SUBTONIC (leading tone)	○	7	vii°
SUBMEDIANT	○	6	vi
SUBDOMINANT (passive)	☾	4	IV

Left: The seven roots of the the seven triads each have a specific spatial relationship to the tonic. The tonic/home (Earth), has great gravity in tonal music, strongly pulling the two bodies closest to it (ii and vii°). The Sun and Moon, a fifth away up or down, have the weakest gravity and can exist as separate, yet related entities.

V negates I, while implying its presence by resolving to it. IV already contains the root of I in its triad, so is more closely related to the tonic than V.

The mediant (middle third) and submediant (lower middle third) have moderate gravity and are weaker stopping points, sharing two tones each with two chords.

ROOT MOVEMENTS

2ND Root moves up or down by a second. Strong movement, no common tones.

3RD Root moves up or down by a third. Gradual movement, two common.

4TH or 5TH Strongest movement, around the circle of fifths. One common tone.

PACHELBEL'S CANON I $-$ V $-$ vi $-$ iii $-$ IV $-$ I $-$ ii $-$ V

HEART AND SOUL I $-$ vi $-$ ii $-$ V

LET IT BE I $-$ V $-$ vi $-$ IV $-$ I $-$ V $-$ IV $-$ I

progression ⟷ *regression*

primary **MAJOR**	I	IV	V	I
secondary **MINOR**		vi	iii	
	(iii)	ii	vii°	(vi)

SUBSTITUTIONS

Above: Upward root movement is progressive. Downward movement tends to be more regressive and relaxed. Most chord progressions are a circular balance of up and down, near and far. Apart from the special relationship between I, IV, and V, the fewer common tones between two chords, the greater the sense of movement.

Left: When reducing secondary chords to their primary function, we can see whether a chord succession is progressing or regressing, active or passive, and thereby gauge the energy and rate of movement.

INSTRUMENTATION
the textures of timbre

Musicologists identify six basic types of musical instrument: membranophones (membranes), chordophones (strings), idiophones (struck), metallophones (metallic), aerophones (air), and electrophones (electronic).

Wind instruments generally have an open end, and often a conical shape to release sound into the air. Wind can be moved through a narrow space to vibrate a reed, or two, or sound can be generated by the buzzing of lips (blowing through a tube), as with brass instruments. Strings can be either plucked or bowed, and can resonate in sympathetic accord with other strings. Percussion instruments move air quickly, abruptly, and noisily, and have membranes and means of striking them. They provide contrast to the smooth, sustained tones of melody and harmony, punctuating with shakes, sizzles, tingles, and rings. All cultures utilize percussion in their music, and many brass and stringed instruments reveal the algorithmic spiral or curvature of pitch. Some cultures also believe instruments contain animal souls that sing when the gut or skin vibrates. Many instruments resemble the structures of the ear, both being part of the vibration duality, instruments generating and the ear receiving. The voice can imitate most (*the basic ranges of male and female voices are shown below*).

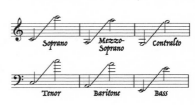

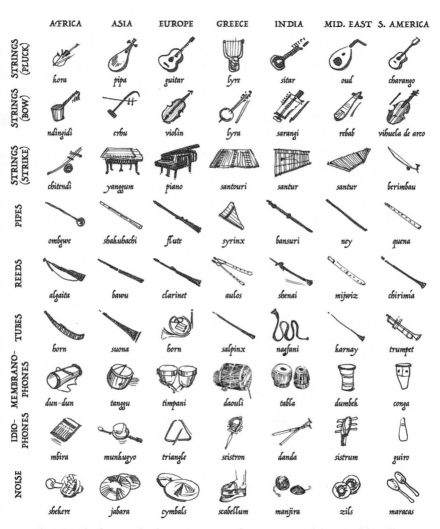

	AFRICA	ASIA	EUROPE	GREECE	INDIA	MID. EAST	S. AMERICA
STRINGS (PLUCK)	kora	pipa	guitar	lyre	sitar	oud	charango
STRINGS (BOW)	ndingidi	erhu	violin	lyra	sarangi	rebab	viþuela de arco
STRINGS (STRIKE)	chitendi	yanggum	piano	santouri	santur	santur	berimbau
PIPES	ombgwe	shakuhachi	flute	syrinx	bansuri	ney	quena
REEDS	algaita	bawu	clarinet	aulos	shenai	mijwiz	chirimia
TUBES	horn	suona	horn	salpinx	nagfani	karnay	trumpet
MEMBRANO-PHONES	dun-dun	tanggu	timpani	daouli	tabla	dumbek	conga
IDIO-PHONES	mbira	munkuzyo	triangle	seistron	danda	sistrum	guiro
NOISE	shekere	jabara	cymbals	scabellum	manjira	zils	maracas

Above: Examples of string, wind, and percussion instruments from various times and places around the world.

23

More Complex Rhythms
dynamics, articulation, elocution, & syncopation

Sounds evolve over time, and *envelopes* (*below*) use three basic phases (inception, continuation, and closure) to characterize different qualities of volume over time. *Staccato* notes have a short and detached quality, *tenuto* notes are slightly lengthened to connect them (in *legato* fashion) to those nearby, while an *accent* indicates a strong start to a tone, emphasizing its initiation.

Piano and *forte* are soft and strong indications used to suggest volume or amplitude. The pianoforte (piano) was so named for its ability to play both loud and soft, in contrast to earlier keyboard instruments, the harpsichord and clavichord, which could not.

Articulations and dynamics in music notation shape passages and contribute to the sense of character and mood, whether playful, doleful, whimsical, or aggressive. Articulations affect the presence of noise in the instrument, acting as consonants upon vowels.

Opposite are shown dotted rhythms, used in triple notation. Notice the dot to the right of the note, rather than above or below it (as with staccato). Rhythms continue to complexify and subdivide in syncopation and polyrhythms (*see too appendix III, page 56*).

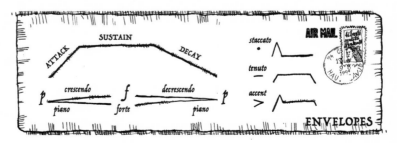

24

DOTTED
NOTES AND RESTS

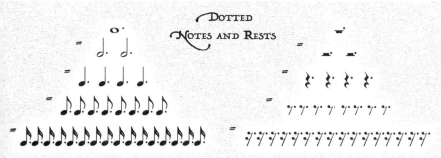

Above: Dotted notes (left) and rests (right). Dotted rhythms are equal to one and a half times the value of the undotted note or rest, and are useful for obtaining triple subdivisions.

Above: A sample bass line in 3/4, illustrating the relationship of three quarters to a dotted half note, both occupying the same amount of time.

Above: In 6/8, three eighth notes are equivalent to two dotted eights, which in turn equal one dotted half.

Right: Tuplets can represent any number of subdivisions, depending upon the metric context in which they appear. Tuplet subdivisions are effectively identical to the subdivisions of frequency in the overtone series. By this point in the notational system, virtually any subdivision of the beat can be notated.

POLYRHYTHMS

Above: Polyrhythms occur whenever different subdivisions of the beat appear together, such as 2 against 3, 5 against 4, 4 against 3, 2 against 5, and so on.

SYNCOPATION

Above: Syncopation is the shifting of strong beats on to weak beats, thus changing our sense of predictability and steadiness. Too much syncopation and we are lost for a pulse. Not enough, and we soon grow bored. Listening to how different cultures push and pull against their metric structures can be tracked largely through the use of syncopation.

FORM AND STRUCTURE
where am I going and how did I get here?

Musical structure tends to unfold in parts or sections. An idea, mood, or motif is first presented before something arrives that changes or contrasts it, while nevertheless relating to it, creating a sense of unity and, ultimately, arrival or return. This unfolding pattern also helps orient the listener in time, so that, using their attention and memory, they can tell where they are in the musical texture. Without it they would be adrift in a sea of unrelated ideas, and some music intentionally is composed this way for that very effect.

Most people go through vicissitudes of emotion in their life, leaving home, going out into the world, having adventures, and ultimately returning home. A life's journey is like a musical composition, born into the world from nothing, living for a time in form and structure, dancing spontaneously on the edge of chaos and order, and then finally returning. In this respect Western music tends to be more linear, Eastern music more cyclical.

Musical time can be visualized as a storyboard (*below*), each segment expressing the essence of a particular character, meaning, intention, and purpose of a section or movement. Frequently these sections are ordered with consideration for the attention span of the listener, in varying degrees of complexity and engagement, like a ceremony involving invocation, meditation, and dance.

BASIC MOLECULAR FORMS OF WESTERN MUSIC

BINARY

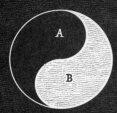

Above: Binary forms are simply two sections that contrast each other to make one whole, AB.

ROUNDED BINARY

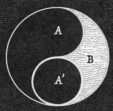

Above: Rounded binary brings back a truncated version of the A, usually just enough to suggest or remind the listener of where they've been, ABA'.

TERNARY

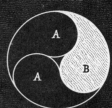

Above: Ternary forms present the A in recapitulation, yielding an - ABA structure.

COSMOLOGICAL DIAGRAMS,

some ancient keys to nuances in the evolution of form - showing how time, space, and manifestation interrelate

Above: The humors, seasons and elements of antiquity. These correspondences illustrate a kind of interrelated dynamism and flow to time, character, personality type, and the human experience.

Above: The Far-Eastern system of elements, demonstrating principles of balance and imbalance, and showing how the flow of time and the elements correspond to interact and influence each other.

MORE COMPLEX HARMONIES
sevenths and their inversions add suspense

Continuing to stack thirds beyond the triad yields major, minor, or diminished sevenths, with their dynamic pull toward the tonic. As the root and fifth of a chord provide architectural structure, the third and seventh provide feeling and flavor, push and pull. Sometimes referred to as *guide tones*, they lead the movement of harmony from chord to chord, adding to the intensity of the forward drive. The presence of two guide tones in a chord maximizes this, e.g., the dominant 7th, whose third and seventh often resolve to the tonic root and third.

Hollow *suspended* chords, where the third is replaced with its junior or senior note, are shown below. Similarly *add* chords take on a color without compromising any of the three basic notes of the triad, the 2, 4, and 6 sweetening the overall sonority.

If the lowest tone is kept constant, as chords move around it, then we are in the presence of a *pedal point*, so named because of the ability of the organ to sustain bass tones played with the feet while changing harmonies played with the hands on the keyboard, keeping a central bottom tone in place, which may or may not be the root of the chord. In fact, a pedal point doesn't have to belong to the chord at all, differentiating it from an inversion.

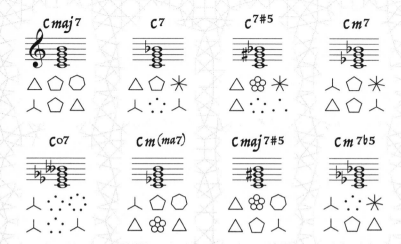

Above: The eight basic seventh chords derived from stacking thirds. Note the interval content of the major chords versus the minor chords, also the open and expansive quality to chords with more perfect and major intervals, and the more closed and contractive quality to chords with diminished and minor intervals. The maj7, m(ma7) and maj7#5 have the most large intervals. The 7#5 and m7 have an equal balance, and the 7, °7, and m7♭5 (also known as half-diminished ø) are made up mostly of smaller intervals.

		C maj7	C7	C7#5	C m7	C o7	C m(ma7)	C maj7#5	C m7♭5
3RD INV	$\begin{smallmatrix}6\\4\\2\end{smallmatrix}$	B	B♭	B♭	B♭	B♭♭	B	B	B♭
2ND INV	$\begin{smallmatrix}6\\4\\3\end{smallmatrix}$	G	G	G#	G♭	G♭	G	G#	G♭
1ST INV	$\begin{smallmatrix}6\\5\\3\end{smallmatrix}$	E	E	E	E♭	E♭	E♭	E	E♭
ROOT	$\begin{smallmatrix}7\\5\\3\end{smallmatrix}$	C	C	C	C	C	C	C	C

Above: Inverted sevenths. The figured bass notation (second column) indicates the intervallic placement of notes above the bass, which in fact indicates the inversion, though the 1, 3, and 5 are assumed and not always written. We still hear the identity and therefore function of the chord as though it were in root position. The brain reassembles the notes into their closest formation, regardless of how the individual notes are voiced, even when spaced openly across octaves (see too page 16).

TONALITY AND MODULATION
there's no place like home

Tonality, or the sense of being in a particular key, is most easily created by sounding the I–IV–V–I pattern (*see pages 20-21*).

The tonic chord has the same function as the tonic note of the scale. It is the place where things begin and end, and to which all things relate. In tonal music the leading tone is always used to point to the tonic, and, as with the circularity of the scale, all other stations of the scale and their chords serve either to strengthen or weaken the relative gravity of the tonic, departing or returning.

The mighty tonic, however, can be destabilized. Chords other than the tonic can be strengthened by the introduction of their respective leading tones (the third of any dominant chord, a half step below a root). Notes outside of the key can make an appearance to point to other roots as possible tonics. The sense of a second key can emerge. If this happens within the appropriate time, and with the repetition of the I–IV–V–I chords of the new key, then a full *modulation* occurs, and a new tonic is formed. Without these affirmations, the movement is temporary, and only a *tonicization* has occurred.

After a time, the ear may become accustomed to the new key, but tonal music often returns to the first by reinstating the changed note, creating the sense that we never really left. Before long, a relationship of keys emerges, reflecting the relationships of chords, which in turn reflect the relationships of the individual tones in the scale.

Authentic ! Plagal . Deceptive ? Half ,

V   I   IV$^6_4$ I   V   vi   IV   I$^6_4$ V

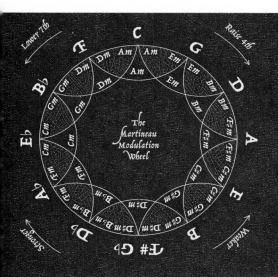

Lower 7th

Raise 4th

C
G
F
D
B♭
A
E♭
E
A♭
B
D♭
G♭ #F

Am Am
Dm Dm Em Em
Gm Gm Am Bm Bm
Cm Gm Dm F#m F#m
Cm Cm C#m C#m
F#m C#m G#m G#m D#m D#m
Bm Bm
G#m B♭m D#m
A♭m B♭m

The
Martineau
Modulation
Wheel

Stronger

Weaker

Left: The circle of fifths is not only a diagram of common tones, but also a diagram of common chords, which can be used to facilitate a modulation (change of key). In the diagram the major keys are on the outside of the circle, while minor triads, the relative minors of the outermost major keys, occupy the interior. Any major chord will also belong to the two scales flanking it on either side.

Example 1: The key of C major shares the chords of A minor and D minor with the key of F major, easily visible in the diagram.

Example 2: The key of E minor shares the chord of C major with the key of D minor.

Raising the 4th of a key acquires the scale of a fifth higher. Lowering the 7th reaches the scale of a fifth below. There are only two half step pairs in the major scale (3-4, 7-8), and they are therefore the most unstable, easily accommodating this kind of key change.

Right: In this basic I-IV-V-I progression, note how the tritone, or diminished fifth formed between the unstable leading tone B and upper F of G7, contracts inward to the stable root and third, joined by the upward movement of the dominant in the bass. This maximizes the finality and reality of the chord in the I position being the true home.

Left: Cadences (endings). A cadence in music works much the same way as punctuation in language. The authentic cadence has a strong degree of finality due to its leading tone and its root resolving to the tonic. The plagal cadence is subtler, lacking the active drive of the dominant, the "A-men" in much European sacred music. A deceptive cadence resolves someplace other than the expected resolution, the tonic, often a surprise. The half cadence is open ended, ending on the dominant, sometimes with an intervening tonic chord in 2nd inversion to heighten the expectation of resolution.

I   IV   V7   I

To Modulate from the Key of X to the key of Y
find a pivot chord that is in both keys and substitute for IV

So On the wheel above, moving clockwise:
Moving 1 click: vi in X is ii in Y OR iii in X is vi in Y
Moving 2 clicks: iii in X is ii in Y
(Moving 3 clicks or more requires borrowing from the parallel minor)

In the key of X: 1 - Pivot - V - 1
In X: 1 - Pivot
In Y: Pivot - V - 1

Example: to change key from G to A and back (use Bm):
G - Bm - D7 - G, G - Bm - E7 - A
A - Bm - E7 - A, A - Bm - D7 - G

31

MODAL, TONAL, DRONAL
world systems and scales

In every musical scale there is a much-used primary set of tones, and a smaller secondary set, used to color the first. Basic primary pentatonic, five-note scales form the backbones of many scales around the world (*below*), the most simple deriving from four consecutive fifths. Other scales follow the gravitational forces of the stations, and use chromatic alteration to communicate tension and emotion. Scales with more half steps can be tighter, filled with introversion, chromatic complexity, and pathos, while more diatonic scales can be extroverted, simple, affirming, and expansive.

There are essentially three kinds of pitch organization. *Modal* music, which does not modulate, uses leading tones liberally, sometimes not at all; harmonic movement is possible, and chords can be borrowed from other scales. In *tonal* music, which does modulate, the five secondary tones not used in the major scale have a relatively fixed relationship to the primary set, determined by the circle of fifths, ♯4, ♭7, ♯5, ♯1, ♭3, each temporarily suggesting the scale to which the secondary tones act as leading tones. These accidentals only last for the measure in which they occur, and are restored in subsequent measures, sometimes followed by a courtesy accidental as a reminder. *Dronal* music has no harmony, the scale itself being the harmonic universe, so the intervals all relate solely to the still point, the drone, with a full chromatic range available.

Major Pentatonic Scales

Minor Pentatonic Scales

MODAL

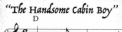

In modal music, the dominant chord need not be major, or even used, and leading tones can occur in positions other than in the standard major/minor. With good harmonic variability and softened tone-tendencies, this is the most common type of harmonic system.

"The Handsome Cabin Boy"

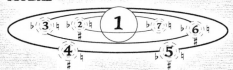

TONAL

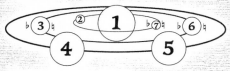

Tonal music involves just two modalities, major and minor. The positions of the half steps are highly organized. The dominant chord is always major, pointing to the tonic with its powerful leading tone (the third of its chord, also the 7th of the scale).

Mozart Sonata in A, KV 331

DRONAL

Dronal music, melodic rather than harmonic in nature, has all the notes of the scale assuming variable roles, taking on importance by interval and repetition, all of them always relating to the central point, resting tone, or drone.

Raga Shivranjani

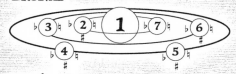

THE THREE MINORS
natural, harmonic, and melodic

The active role of leading tones in harmonic music creates complexities for minor keys. The natural dominant chord in minor is not a major chord, and the need for a leading tone necessitates altering it, and the scale from which it is built.

In the case of *natural minor*, we are in the presence of the Aeolian mode, which occurs naturally as the relative to any major scale, started a third lower. Raising the third in the dominant chord, the seventh of the scale, creates *harmonic minor*, altered for harmonic purposes. The scale that results from this, however, contains an audible gap between the flatted minor 6th and the natural major 7th, an augmented second, which does not always work melodically, sounding like an interval from non–Western music. To smooth out this melodic gap, the 6th scale degree is also altered, raised, so that the ascent in minor resembles a major scale in its upper four notes. This is *melodic minor*, which is sometimes said to have two forms: ascending and descending, raising and lowering the 6th and 7th accordingly. In fact, descending melodic minor is identical to natural minor. Triads of the three minors are shown below.

Natural minor

i · ii° · III · iv · v · VI · VII · i

Harmonic minor

i · ii° · III⁺ · iv · V · VI · vii° · i

Melodic minor (ascending)

i · ii · III⁺ · IV · V · vi° · vii° · i

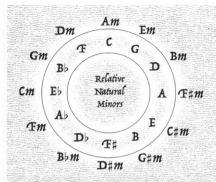

Opposite page: These three minor scales are used interchangeably depending upon the composer's needs, and adhere to basic rules about the use of chromaticism in the minor mode. These scales, like major/Ionian, can be used as starting points to generate others, so in fact there are seven modes of harmonic minor and seven modes of melodic minor (shown below).

Left: Natural minor is identical to a major scale a minor third above. So A minor and C major are in fact the same notes, shifted a third apart. Natural minor, being Aeolian, already shares the same pitches as its relative major, Ionian, therefore they share the same key signature (see page 11).

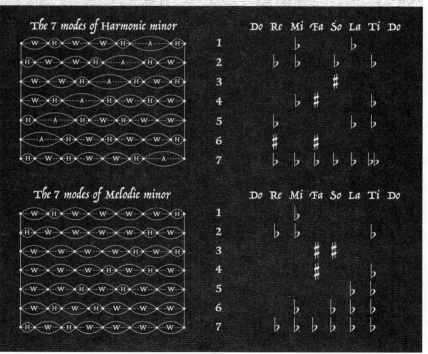

35

MORE INTERVALS
the big get bigger and the small get smaller

Just as chords are invertible, so too are their constituent intervals. 3rds invert to become 6ths, and 7ths become 2nds. Inverted major intervals become minor, inverted diminished intervals become augmented, and vice versa. Inverted intervals have the same basic function as their non-inverted counterparts, but possess a greater sense of uncertainty. Composers play with them by further raising and lowering them. For example, extending a major 6th yields the interval of an augmented 6th, identical in sound to a minor 7th, but functioning quite differently. Remember that spelling counts, and that a minor 7th tends to resolve inward, while an augmented 6th tends to resolve outward—big gets bigger and small gets smaller. Similarly, contracting a minor 7th yields a diminished 7th, the same as a major 6th, but again functioning wholly differently. As a major 6th is likely to fall by a whole step to the 5th, or rise to the major 7th, a diminished 7th almost always falls by a half step. Spelling and syntax indicate behavior and directionality.

Shown below are the only three possible *octatonic* or diminished scales, since they are symmetrical. They fall into the repeating pattern of half-whole or whole-half. Also shown are the only two whole-tone scales, built entirely of whole steps. They can evoke a mysterious sense of ambiguity and the unknown.

The three diminished scales
and
The two whole-tone scales

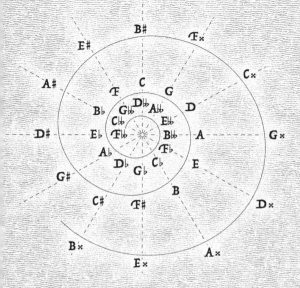

Left: Enharmonicism & Chromaticism. Combining the circle of fifths with the spiral of fifths produces all of the possible 35 spellings for the 12 notes. Remember there are 7 members of the scale, ABCDEFG, and 5 chroma (colors) for each. The outermost and innermost spellings are rarely used (B✗, E✗, F♭♭, C♭♭). Whenever a chromatic alteration must be made to a scale, an accidental is correspondingly used (a lowered flat is double flat, a raised flat is natural, a lowered sharp is natural, a raised natural is sharp, and a raised sharp is double sharp).

This diagram is of equivalence between spellings and assumes equal temperament. It should not be confused with a common diagram demonstrating tuning problems created by the Pythagorean Comma (not covered in this book - see Harmonograph, by Anthony Ashton).

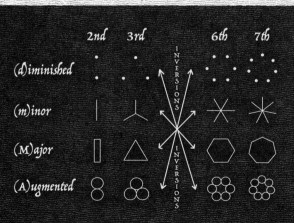

Left: The imperfect consonances (3rds and 6ths) and dissonances (2nds and 7ths) occasionally come in two extreme forms beyond major and minor. Chromatically extending a major interval further turns it into an augmented interval. Likewise further contracting a minor interval makes it diminished, just as a perfect interval becomes diminished when contracted.

Complex and chromatically rich music sometimes will use these enhanced or stretched intervals to push and pull with even more energy against the overall tonal structure.

Further Melodic Elements
epigrammatic development

Humans are fundamentally pattern-based beings, and artists worldwide, visual and acoustic, have used this fact to manipulate audiences for centuries. An idea or epigram is articulated, before undergoing a series of transformations, being reinforced or denied. The unfolding of this drama of denial and acceptance is the narrativity of music, and is played out in three basic ways:

Repetition, or thesis. The easiest thing for an epigram to do is to assert itself, and this is accomplished by repetition. Repetitions are helpful because they are highly orienting for the audience in the context of a given narrative. They are the anchors of time.

Contrast, or antithesis. The drama begins. A new epigram is presented, possibly seeming to contradict the previous one, and creating the tension of a new set of opposites. A completely contrasting epigram, with no epigrammatic transference, is a denial.

Variation, or synthesis. A reconciliation of the two poles of repetition and contrast, sometimes viewed as a fulcrum (*below*).

Melodies, songs, and symphonies all use these three degrees of epigrammatic transference; from total (repetition), through partial or transformative (variation), to none (contrast). The mind absorbs the meaning of each new idea, comparing it to recent and distant events. Attempting to cognize the parts produces anticipation, which may be affirmed or denied. Narrative artists exploit this faculty to create their books and movies, melodies, and rhythms.

38

Species Counterpoint

1st species: Note against note. Only consonances are permitted. Careful avoidance of parallel leaps or steps, especially to a perfect interval, except at a cadence.

2nd species: Two notes against one. Passing tones make their appearance, as dissonances which are permitted only on weak beats. The contrapuntal line can start on a rest.

Third Species: Four (or three) notes against one. Passing tones, neighbor tones, and now escape tones can be used, still adhering to consonances on strong beats.

Fourth Species: Suspensions—offset notes. Consonance is prepared on a weak beat, and when the pitch in the cantus firmus changes, a dissonance is created by the sustained tone on a strong beat, and resolved by a step downward.

Above: Species Counterpoint, a system of rules for writing polyphonic music, dating back to the 16th century. The cantus firmus, or bottom line, is joined by a new melodic line on top. fifth species is the combination of the previous four, known as florid counterpoint. Counterpoint is the simultaneity of melodies, each line running independently of the others horizontally, and aligning to make harmonic sense vertically (often at strong parts of the meter, to convey the harmonic framework). The four-part texture of soprano, alto, tenor, bass in contrapuntal music later became melody, bass line, and "inner voices". The highest voice became the most melodically important, the others taking on a more supporting role, eventually becoming chords, with a collective identity of their own. This more homophonic texture is the "melody and accompaniment" with which we are so familiar. There are three types of contrapuntal motion: parallel, contrary, and oblique.

Above: Theme from Beethoven's 9th Symphony, showing symmetrical nature of epigrammatic melodic movements.

COMPLEX CHORD PROGRESSIONS
getting out of the box

To develop a richer harmonic palette and get out of the I–IV–V–I box, a more complex structure can be developed by borrowing chords from a parallel scale, thus facilitating longer excursions.

Because it is the root of a chord that imparts its functionality, we can freely substitute other chords built upon the same scale degree (*opposite top*) and still preserve the harmonic essence. So a major subdominant (IV) can be substituted for a minor one (iv), or a minor mediant (iii) can be replaced with a major mediant (♭III) and its inflections (♭III+). As long as basic cadences occasionally occur to reinforce a tonic, chords can be borrowed relatively freely.

The dominant seventh chord is well–suited for substitution because of its symmetrical tritone (*see below*). When the root shifts by a tritone, the 3rd and 7th of each chord exchange places. The spelling of this interval changes enharmonically to preserve the syntax, but the sound is the same. In fact, as we move around the circle of fifths with seventh chords, the 3rd and 7th of each chord exchange places and slip and slide by steps, often referred to as step progressions or guide tones, a reciprocity that maximizes the forward drive of harmonic motion. In most chords, it is the root, 3rd and 7th that are sufficient to communicate the harmonic function, so when voicing chords, the 5th can frequently be omitted, since it only reinforces the tonic structurally. If, however, the 5th is altered (♯ or ♭, augmented or diminished), then its color is included as well.

Scale Degree	1	2	3	4	5	6	7	8
Major	C	Dm	Em	F	G	Am	B°	C
	I	ii	iii	IV	V	vi	vii°	I
Natural Minor	Cm	D°	Eb	Fm	Gm	Ab	Bb	Cm
	i	ii°	bIII	iv	v	bVI	bVII	i
Harmonic Minor	Cm	D°	Eb+	Fm	G	Ab	B°	Cm
	i	ii°	bIII+	iv	V	bVI	vii°	i
Melodic Minor	Cm	Dm	Eb+	F	G	A°	B°	Cm
	i	ii	bIII+	IV	V	vi°	vii°	i
Secondary Dominants	C^7	D^7	E^7	F^7	G^7	A^7	B^7	C^7
	V^7/IV	V^7/V	V^7/vi	$V^7/bVII$		V^7/ii	V^7/iii	V^7/IV
Minor secondary Dominants	.	.	Eb^7	.	.	Ab^7	Bb^7	.
			V^7/bVI			V^7/bII	$V^7/bIII$	

Above: A table of substitutions. Secondary dominants act like the primary dominant in that they possess a tritone, and suggest a resolution a fourth up or fifth down. They require a chromatic alteration to the basic scale in use. The new leading tone that results temporarily suggests an alternate key or scale, but this is usually brief, either occurring as a passing chord, or as a tonicization. The presence of borrowed chords weakens the strength of the tonic, but often provides a lovely shading or color, partly due to their violating our expectations about which chords we expect to hear in a given key.

Amazing Grace

I	V^7/IV	IV	I
I	I^6	V	V^7
I	V^7/IV	IV	I
I^6_4	V^7	IV^6	I

Greensleeves

i	bVII	bVI	V^7
i	bVII	bVI - V^7	i
bIII	bVII	bVI	V^7
bIII	bVII	bVI - V^7	i

The well-known song "Amazing Grace" uses inversions, and a secondary dominant, in this case the V of the subdominant (IV). It sounds much like the I chord, only with an added 7th, pointing upward by a fourth. In "Greensleeves" we have a truly modal harmonic progression, borrowing freely from the parallel major, and briefly pointing to the relative major in the third and fourth phrases. There are many ways to harmonize these songs, these examples present only one possibility.

AROUND THE WORLD
in four songs

Every system of musical notation is essentially a set of instructions for the implementation of sounds through time. In each case they are a kind of timeline, tracking sonic events, and in the case of songs, their marriage to words. Lines, dashes, slashes, curves, numbers, letters, dots, and circles all are used to mirror the up and down inflections, gestures, and shapes of melodies.

Earlier in history, music was an entirely oral tradition, much like storytelling, another narrative art form. As humanity spread and grew, new methods were needed to communicate music to more people. Eventually, notation helped bring music into the homes of everyday musicians, and preserve it for future generations to enjoy. This parallels the development of the printing press, with the same advantages facilitated by that invention. Since we all have basically the same set of musical and linguistic sounds available to us, these various notation systems (*four examples shown opposite*) have a great deal in common. They all indicate the placement of rhythms, the association of notes with syllables of language, and the melodic contours, as well as the overall form of the composition.

In India, because of the complexities of tuning, there are 22 possible tones, allowing for purer acoustic relationships, with simple whole-number ratios between them. Scales are derived from the overall set, depending upon the *raga* desired. Each 7-note *that* or *mela* has a distinct flavor, not unlike the Western modes with its *swaras* (*Sa, Re, Ga, Ma, Pa, Da* and *Ni*) born from the twenty-two *shrutis*.

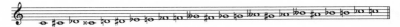

Bhatkhande notation - Indian
Early 20th century
This is used to indicate the rag, tal, and tempo, as well as melody and lyrics for Indian music.

Song of Seikilos - Greek
c. 200 BC - 100 AD
Likely the oldest surviving music notation in the world, this example indicates the lyrics and the basic melodic outline.

Jianpu - Chinese
18th century
This system uses numbers corresponding to pitches of the scale and dots and lines to indicate durations and rests, with lyrics streaming underneath.

Medieval Europe
13th century
A musical staff is used here, much like contemporary staves in Western music, with squares and lines to indicate pitch and rhythm, and lyrics streaming underneath.

Advanced Harmonies
rascals and spices

Because the dominant chord is the chord of hope and anticipation, chromatic added tones are easily accommodated to add more intervallic complexity. This in turn strengthens the urge to resolve, which can either be fulfilled or denied for the manipulation of tension and release. Extensions can also be added to any of the four chord qualities: major, minor, diminished, or augmented.

It is the non–chord tones or non–station notes that provide the coloring of the essential chord qualities. When they are voiced next to nearby stations, they are considered an "added" effect. When these color tones are transposed an octave higher, they become the 9ths, 11ths, and 13ths, which are generally arrived at by stacking thirds. From the root, we pass through the 3rd, 5th, 7th, 9th, 11th, 13th, and conceivably beyond (*opposite top*). These pitch arrangements can yield some startlingly complex harmonic structures, yet the bottom three members of the stack still retain their identity, and imbue the whole edifice with a basic flavor. Music since the end of the 19th century has explored these expanded harmonic possibilities, particularly jazz.

Sixth chords are a category of harmonies with chromatic alterations that don't fit into the usual parallel major/minor borrowing structure, sometimes referred to as vagrants. They are alterations of the subdominant chord, decorating the dominant.

An example of chord notation with extensions is shown below.

MISTY (A)   E♭maj7 | B♭m9   E♭13 | A♭maj7 | A♭m9   D♭13#11
             E♭maj7 C7#9 | Fm7   B♭7 | Gm7   C7♭9 | Fm7   B♭13♭9

Left. Tones can be stacked on top of a chord beyond the root, 3rd, 5th, 7th, and octave, further complicating and enriching its structure and intervallic flavor. The higher these tones, the less functional and more colorful they become. As we continue to stack, we assume each new note below is included, so a 9th chord includes the 7th. If the extension is not stacked, then it is "added" (see page 28). Some examples are shown above.

Above: Multiple resolutions of the diminished 7th chord. Because the diminished chord is completely symmetrical, comprised entirely of minor thirds and tritones, any and all of its pitches can function as potential roots. In each example the same four notes in each inversion yield a slightly different enharmonic spelling of the same diminished chord, preserving the syntax of thirds. Each tone has an opportunity to be a leading tone, and resolve upward by a half step, and can therefore resolve to four possible chords. These resulting four roots themselves in turn spell out a diminished chord, built from consecutive minor thirds (E-G-Bb-Db).

Above: Resolutions of the various altered 6th chords. The Italian, French, and German versions function like secondary dominants, substituting for the dominant. In the Italian, the augmented sixth is created between the Ab and the F#, since they resolve outward. The German chord is in possession of a perfect fifth, while the unusual flavor of the French is due to the lowered fifth, making a chord with two major thirds and two diminished fourths or tritones, a harmonically suggestive symmetrical chord. The Neapolitan version functions like the subdominant, most often a bII chord, popular in minor.

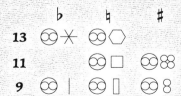

Left: Just as the intermediary tones 2, 4, and 6 come in certain flavors, their correlates, up one octave, the 9th, 11th, and 13th, come in the same flavors, lowered, natural, or raised. All tones above the octave correspond to the tones within the octave, with seven steps added.

ADVANCED FORMS
getting organized

Musical forms are often mixed and matched, with historical hybrids commonplace. Molecular binary and ternary units can be combined and compounded to yield more complex structures, these storyboard squares being used flexibly as general templates.

Attention tends to be highest at the outset of a composition, so music often contains the most intellectually demanding material at this time. An initial tempo will be lively (allegro), perhaps preceded by a slower introduction. Middle movements are often contemplative and reflective, a break from the first movement. Finales are generally light, playful, and dance-like. This common template derives from Baroque dance suites, which were an assemblage of these different moods, variously extroverted and introverted.

There is a general format in the rhetorical unfolding of a complex form: exposition, contrast, development, and summation, and occasionally transformation. Often there is a climax, or a series of them with progressively higher peaks and summits, finally followed by a coming down, unraveling, or denouement.

Sonata form reached its apex in the Classical era and is still in use today. It possesses a fixed relationship of keys and themes. After an introduction, a theme is presented, followed by a contrasting theme. The two themes are then deconstructed and combined in a development section, often tonally unstable or ambiguous, after which the two themes return, a recapitulation. However, the second theme, while first presented in the dominant (or at times another related key) now returns in the tonic key, tying together the journey of contrast and differentiation.

46

Exposition ——————→ Development Recapitulation ——————→

Intro	X	Y	(XY)	X	Y	Coda
	Tonic	Dominant	Modulate	Tonic	Tonic	

SONATA: A very specific structure. The Y theme first occurs transposed, often to the dominant, and upon returning is then restored to the tonic.

Q R S T U V W

THROUGH-COMPOSED: Each section is new and different. Generally little or no repetition.

X P X Q X R X

RONDO: A main theme alternates with intervening contrasting sections.

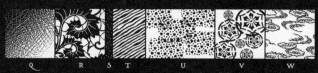

X Y Z Y X

ARCH: A palindromic structure with its keystone in the center.

X Xa Xb Xc Xd Xe

THEME & VARIATIONS: A main theme, follwed by sections generated and derived from it.

PUTTING IT ALL TOGETHER
conceive, create, and compose

Perceiving music as an unfolding of epigrams, molecules of meaning, unities of opposites, allows for a new appreciation of its narrative quality. It becomes possible to perceive or even measure the rate of transference as the music unfolds, and to appreciate more deeply the way in which the drama is reinforced or denied, by seeing the very mechanisms by which it accomplishes those things. Degrees of contrast and repetition can be measured, and most importantly variation and transformation can be understood as a kind of evolution. Like the stations of the scale and the pulse, epigrams also have gravity, and what happens in between them communicates part of the drama of the intentionality of the transference; its story, its plight. And in the most skillful hands, our souls follow suit.

In melody these nuances are most easily heard in the large variety of scales found around the world. Although they all possess some forms of fifths and thirds, it is the notes between that convey the real meaning, tension and release, the distances of those "between" tones, and how they are rhythmically placed. Again, in rhythm, though there is often a predictable pulse, what happens in the spaces in between is much more complex, and can suggest tensions against the different beats, based on their relative distances from the pulse. These epigrams, melodic and rhythmic, can then be arranged into larger coherent structures, compositions, also unifying opposites, and so music is born.

The music we love is the drama of the transference of epigrams, opposites in interplay, unfolding, repeating, contrasting, and most importantly, varying, through melody, harmony, and rhythm.

Above: A Chopin Prelude. The key is A, the tempo Andantino, a little walking pace, the meter ¾, to be played dolce (sweetly). Curved lines (slurs) indicate the phrases. The melody begins with a pickup on beat three, and commences in the first complete measure. An E⁷ chord suggests the key of A. The C♯ in measure 1 is an appoggiatura, along with its dotted rhythm followed by three repeated chords, the primary epigram for this little piece. On beat three of measure 2 is a pair of escape tones, followed by a pair of appoggiaturas in measure 3. The harmony proceeds from V to I, completing one full phrase. Measure 5 again discloses the first epigram, with the appoggiatura on beat 1, doubled, now with a dominant 9th chord, elaborating the earlier dominant 7th. The 3rd, G♯, is now missing. The second phrase completes the first by measure 8. Measure 9 begins the first phrase again, a literal repetition. Measure 11 sounds much like measure 3, voiced slightly higher in range, but resolves to the surprising secondary dominant F♯⁷, the densest chord in the piece. Now it is time to head home. In measure 13 there is a passing tone on beat 1, followed by the falling 7th of B minor, and a voicing of the dominant 9th, this time with the third, G♯, included (thank you, Chopin). The last phrase of the last two bars is the final gesture, widely spaced, with the tonic at the top, letting us know the music has indeed finished.

GLOSSARY OF TERMS

ACCIDENTAL - *Any of the five symbols (bb, b, nat, #, x) that lower or raise a pitch by one or two semitones, usually used to alter or restore a key.*

ADD - *An intermediary or non-chord tone added to a chord for flavoring or color, usually a 2nd, 4th, 6th, 9th, 11th, or 13th.*

ANACRUSIS - *A pickup or upbeat, preceding a metrically strong downbeat.*

APPOGGIATURA - *A dissonant tone that occurs on a strong beat, and then resolves to a consonance or chord tone, it "leans" against the consonance and then relaxes into it.*

AUGMENTED - *Used to describe an interval or chord. With intervals, it indicates a perfect or major interval raised one semitone, with chords, it indicates a major triad with a raised fifth.*

BINARY FORM - *A basic A-B structure in musical form, often each contrasting section repeats.*

CADENCE - *Three or more tones or assembly of notes and rhythms that suggest a sense of closure, pause, or finality to a musical phrase or section.*

CAESURA - *A pause or rest.*

CAMBIATA - *A dissonance formula that is a double neighbor tone, effectively a tone and its two flanking tones, above and below.*

CHORD - *Three or more tones sounding together as an independent entity. They are often spelled largely in thirds, the primary core being a triad.*

CHROMATIC - *colorful, used to indicate music using semitones, accidentals, or the entire 12-tone collection, contrasted with diatonic.*

CLEF - *A symbol placed at the beginning of the staff that indicates where pitches are to be placed on the lines and spaces of the staff, the three types being the G-clef, F-clef, and C-clef.*

CONSONANCE - *The relative stability of a musical interval, generally not requiring resolution, contrasted with dissonance. Most often octaves, fifths, fourths, thirds, and sixths.*

COUNTERPOINT - *The simultaneity of independent lines, which are coherent horizontally and vertically, adhering to strict rules about consonance and dissonance, with historical variance.*

CRESCENDO - *A gradual increasing in volume and intensity, indicated by an expanding hairpin in musical notation.*

DECRESCENDO - *A gradual decreasing in volume and intensity, indicated by a contracting hairpin in musical notation.*

DIATONIC - *A scale comprised of seven different contiguous tones, with a specific relationship of whole and half steps, often used to describe major and minor. Contrasted with chromatic. Also describes music that adheres to this scale.*

DIMINISHED - *Used to describe a musical interval or chord, either the lowering of a perfect interval by one semitone, or a triad with a minor third and diminished fifth.*

DISSONANCE - *One or more musical intervals that suggest instability, most often seconds and sevenths, and tend to require some form of resolution to a consonance.*

DOMINANT - *The scale degree a fifth above a root or tonic of a key, also a powerful station of the scale, that often suggests its own resolution, back to the tonic. Often it is present in a cadence.*

DRONAL - *Music that is primarily melodic and rhythmic, lacking harmonic movement, with all scale tones relating to a drone or still point.*

EPIGRAM - *As used in this book, a musical motive or idea that has just enough particularity and individuality to constitute a recognizable shape and identity, often functioning as a basic building block of an entire composition.*

ÉSCHAPPÉE - *Escape tone, a dissonance on a weak part of the beat that is approached by step, followed by a leap to a consonance in the opposite direction.*

EXTENSION - *Tones above the octave added to a chord to enrich its overall color without altering its function, always a 9th, 11th, or 13th. Also known as a "tension."*

FLAT - *A symbol used to indicate a lowering of a natural by one semitone. Also used to describe a tone that is tuned slightly under pitch.*

FORTE - *A symbol in dynamics used to indicate music to be played "strongly" or loudly, contrasted with piano.*

FRICATIVE - *A friction-based consonant in spoken language, such as F, V, H, and TH.*

GUIDE TONE - *Usually the 3rd and 7th of a chord, acting as leading tones that maximize the forward motion of a harmonic progression.*

HALF STEP - *See Semitone.*

HARMONIC MINOR - *One of the three types of minor scales, in which the 6th scale degree is lowered and the 7th scale degree is raised, to allow for the dominant chord to be major. Thus it has the interval of an augmented second between the 6th and 7th.*

HARMONICS - *Each of the component tones of the overtones series, which imbue the lowest tone, the fundamental, with timbre or color, each being mathematically related to it in whole-number ratios, 1x, 2x, 3x, gradually increasing in frequency. Many string and wind instruments can be played in such a way to reveal these softer upper tones.*

HARMONY - *The relationship of a vertical arrangement of tones when sounding together, also a chord, and the way in which chords relate and are organized through time.*

ICTUS - *A metric accent or strong beat, often a downbeat.*

INTERVAL - *The distance between two pitches.*

INVERSION - *With musical intervals, it is the operation of taking the bottom note and placing it at the top, so a 2nd yields a 7th, 3rd a 6th, 4th a 5th, and so on. In harmony, it indicates that a note other than the root of the chord is in the bass.*

KEY - *A collection of pitches that reinforce one note as a tonic. There are 12 major and 12 minor keys in Western music, each built upon one of the 12 notes, with sharps and flats added accordingly to preserve whole steps and half steps.*

KEY SIGNATURE - *The global instruction indicating which notes are to be raised or lowered in a composition to preserve and express a particular scale, placed at the beginning of a staff before the meter and after the clef.*

LEADING TONE - *The seventh scale degree of any scale, most often a half step below the tonic.*

LEGATO - *A musical instruction to play the notes in a connected and smooth fashion, with no breaks in between.*

MAJOR - *In describing musical intervals, this indicates the 2nd, 3rd, 6th, and 7th as they occur naturally in the major scale. In describing chords, a triad that is made up of a perfect fifth, and in between a major third, placed above the root. Contrasted with minor. Also describes an overall scale or key flavor, always referring to the third of the scale.*

MEASURE/BAR - *A parcel of musical time, segmented by the meter, in which one complete grouping is delimited. In notation, a measure is separated by a line on either side.*

MEDIANT - *The third scale degree of any scale.*

MELISMATIC - *Vocal music that has two or more pitches assigned to one syllable.*

MELODIC MINOR - *One of the three minors, in this scale the 6th and 7th scale degrees are altered to appear as they do in the major scale to heighten the upward movement to the tonic. Often a descending version also exists as an unaltered version of the natural minor.*

MELODY - *The succession of tones in time, arranged in a meaningful pattern, which can be of varying lengths.*

METER - *A pattern of rhythmic groupings indicated by a fraction, in which the numerator indicates the number of beats per measure, and the denominator indicates the type of subdivisions to receive the beat (quarter, eighth, sixteenth). The two basic forms of meter are duple and triple.*

MINOR - *In describing musical intervals, this indicates a major interval lowered by a semitone or half step. In harmony, a chord that is made up of a perfect fifth, and in between a minor third, placed above the root. Contrasted with major. Also describes an overall scale or key flavor. Western music identifies three types of minors, natural, harmonic, and melodic.*

MODAL - *Music that utilizes scales other than major and minor, such as Phrygian, Dorian, Lydian, etc. (see pp. 8-9). Often this type of music does not modulate.*

MODULATION - *A changing of key or scale in which the tonal center moves, and the accidentals required for one scale are introduced to alter the previous one. This is most easily conveyed by a I-IV-V-I harmonic formula.*

NATURAL - *An accidental that cancels a sharp, flat, double sharp, or double flat, corresponding to the white notes on the piano.*

NATURAL MINOR - *The Aeolian mode, this is the minor scale without any alterations to its 6th or 7th scale degrees.*

NEIGHBOR TONE - *A non-chord tone that exists above or below a chord tone as a temporary dissonance and decoration, usually on a weak beat.*

OCTATONIC - *An eight-note scale, most often referring to diminished scales.*

OVERTONE SERIES - *A natural acoustic phenomenon occurring wherever a vibration of a string or air through a pipe occurs. The length of the vibration increasingly subdivides, yielding vibrations or frequencies higher in sound than the largest vibration. These arrange together to form timbre, and communicate the identity of the sound. Also responsible for the vowels in spoken language.*

PASSING TONE - *An intermediary tone between two chord tones, usually a dissonance, occurring on a weak beat.*

PENTATONIC - *A five-note scale, most often referring to the first five fifths when arranged together, 1-2-3-5-6. Also the black notes on the piano.*

PERFECT - *A musical interval of an octave, 5th, 4th, (and unison), which most closely resemble the first acoustic intervals of the overtone series.*

PIANO - *A musical instruction indicating music to be played "softly" or quietly. Contrasted with forte.*

PLOSIVES - *An explosive sounding consonant in spoken language, often a B, P, D, G, or Q.*

POLYRHYTHMS - *The simultaneous use of two different rhythmic patterns that do not directly relate to one-another, also called "cross rhythms."*

REGISTER - *A specific region of the entire pitch range of an instrument, voice, or piece of music.*

RHYTHM - *The temporal arrangement of movement, quite often possessing a pulse.*

ROOT - *The bottommost pitch of a triad or chord, which conveys its function and identity in the context of a harmonic progression. It is always discoverable by arranging the notes into closely voiced thirds.*

ROUNDED BINARY - *A musical structure in the form ABA, where the last A is a shorter, truncated version of the first.*

SEMITONE - *A half step, the smallest interval in Western traditional music. Two adjacent notes on the piano, whether white or black.*

SHARP - *A symbol used to indicate a raising of a natural by one semitone. Also used to describe a tone that is tuned slightly above pitch.*

SIBILANTS - *A type of fricative consonant in spoken language, at higher frequencies, often resembling a hissing sound, such as S, and Z.*

SONATA - *As used in this book, specifically a formal procedure which presents two contrasting themes, the second being in a key other than the tonic (often the dominant), followed by a modulatory and free development section, and then a recapitulation in which the two themes are presented again, and the second theme is restored to the tonic key.*

STACCATO - *A musical instruction indicating notes to be played in a detached fashion, usually marked by a small dot above or below the note.*

SUBDOMINANT - *The fourth scale degree, a fifth below the tonic, and a whole step below the dominant. It often functions as a departure from the tonic and a preparation for the dominant.*

SUBMEDIANT - *The sixth scale degree of any scale, a third below the tonic.*

SUBTONIC - *The seventh scale degree of any scale, most often a whole tone below the tonic (see Leading tone).*

SUPERTONIC - *The second scale degree of any scale, a step above the tonic.*

SUSPENSION - *A chord in which the third is held or suspended from resolving as the rest of the tones resolve, prepared in the previous chord. In modern music, the suspension needs no preparation, nor resolution.*

SYLLABIC - *Vocal music that has only one pitch assigned to a syllable.*

SYNCOPATION - *A rhythmic procedure by which strong beats are shifted to weak beats, temporarily obscuring the sense of pulse or meter. The use of syncopation is one of the strongest indicators of musical styles around the world.*

TEMPO - *The rate or speed of a musical performance through time.*

TENUTO - *A musical instruction indicating notes that are to be played in a sustained or extended fashion, usually marked by a line or dash above or below the note.*

TERNARY - *A musical structure in the form ABA, where the last A is generally a complete repetition of the first.*

TONAL - *Music using the principles of tonic-dominant relationships, predominantly the major and minor systems prevalent in Western music.*

TONIC - *The home or resting point of a scale, the strongest point of gravity to which all other tones relate, the first scale degree.*

TONICIZATION - *A temporary support of and pointing to a tonal center other than the tonic, but not firmly confirmed, which only occurs in a modulation.*

TRANSPOSITION - *A moving of the notes of a composition up or down from one key to another, while keeping the relative intervals intact.*

TRIAD - *A three-note structure, arranged in thirds, and resulting in one of the four chord types: major, minor, diminished, or augmented.*

TRITONE - *A diminished 5th, or augmented 4th, made of three whole tones, or six semitones. The largest symmetrical interval in the Western scale, it divides the octave perfectly in half, and is its own inversion. Often utilized in a dominant 7th chord (represented by the fourth and seventh scale degrees of a major scale), it has a powerful forward drive toward resolution by contraction or expansion, and is in fact the liberating force that unlocks the puzzle of tonality by pushing and pulling into and out of one key into another.*

WHOLE TONE - *Also a whole step, comprised of two half steps or semitones.*

51

APPENDIX I - BASIC NOTATION

Staff – the lattice or matrix that holds notes and rests in place

Treble Clef – also known as G clef, its inner spiral encircles G

Bass Clef – also known as F clef, its inner spiral encircles F

Alto Clef – also known as C clef, wherever the loops meet is middle C

Tenor Clef – also known as C clef, middle C is a 3rd higher than Alto Clef

Percussion Clef – for rhythmic notation, non-pitched instruments

Ledger Lines – lines drawn above and below the staff to extend the pitch range

Coda – a signpost indicating an ending, placed in the score, and at the end

Segno – a signpost indicating a return, often after the beginning, as a D.S. (Da Segno)

Repeat – like parenthesis, indicating start and end of repeated music

Repeat – repeat previous bar

Fermata – placed over a note or rest, indicating time stopping momentarily

Trill – an ornament, oscillating repeatedly with the note above or below

Trill – an ornament, oscillating once or twice with the note above or below

Up Bow – for strings, an upward bow direction

Down Bow – for strings, a downward bow direction

Martellato – (very marked) a strong accent or punctuation

Staccato – a brief, detached articulation

Harmonic – indicates an overtone to be played in place of the fundamental

Accent/Marcato – a general demarcation, not as strong as martellato

Tenuto – an indication to maximize and connect the duration of the note

8va/8vb – play notes an octave higher or lower than written note

15va/15vb – play notes two octaves higher or lower than written note

stem

Dotted Note – adds half the value of the note to the note

Double Dot – adds half the value of the note to the note, and then half of that

Arpeggiando – the chord is to be rolled

Grace Note – smaller, unmeasured decorative note, can come in groups

Tremolo – indicates a note repeating or vibrating rapidly

beam

Slur – legato phrasing, connected notes. For strings: one bow direction. For winds and brass: one breath

notehead

Tie – unites the durations of two notes together into one across a beat or barline

1st and 2nd Endings – these are form indications that provide for alternate endings for repeated music

Rhythm Slash – often used in lead sheets, indicates the flow of beats

Cut Time/Alla Breve – indicates 2/2

pp Pianissimo, very soft

p Piano, soft

mp Mezzo-piano, medium soft

mf Mezzo-forte, medium strong

f Forte, strong, loud

ff Fortissimo, very strong

sfz Sforzando – a forceful accent

Crescendo – increasingly louder

Decrescendo – increasingly softer

Ped. ✶ Pedal – used for piano notation, indicates to depress and release the sustain pedal

Double Bar (final) – indicates the ending of a score

Double Bar – indicates the ending of a section

Common Time – indicates 4/4

sixty-fourth hemidemisemiquaver	thirty-second demisemiquaver	sixteenth semiquaver	eighth quaver	quarter crotchet	half minim	whole semibreve	US UK

Appendix II - Scales

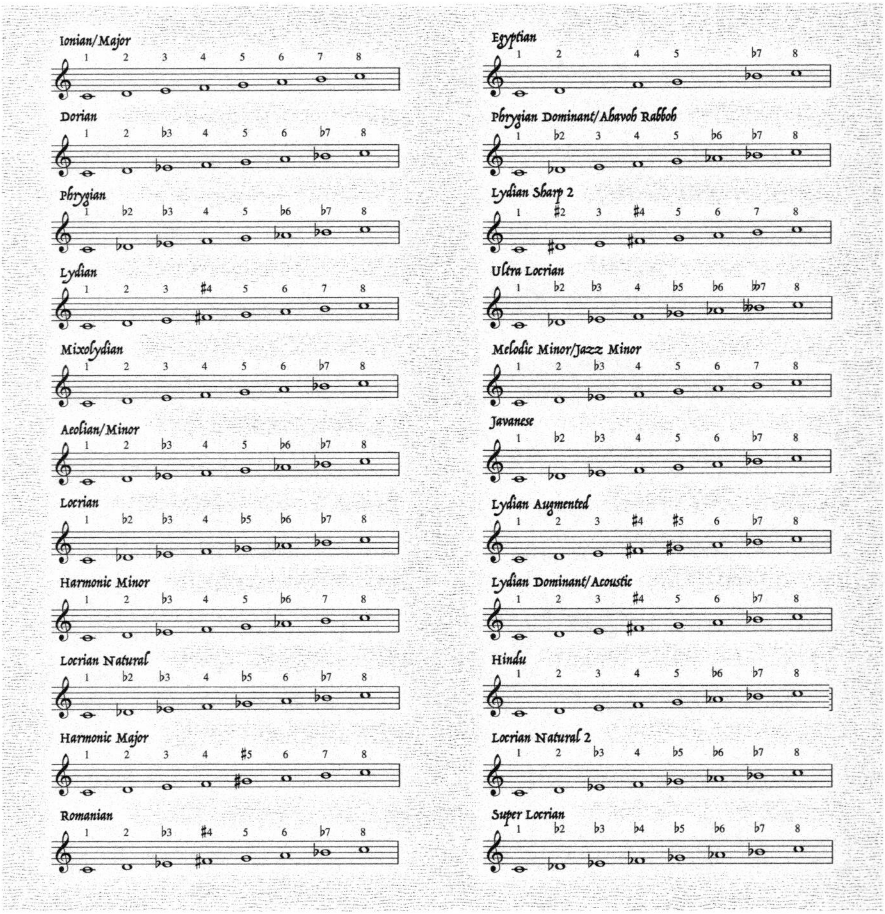

APPENDIX III - SELECTED RHYTHMS

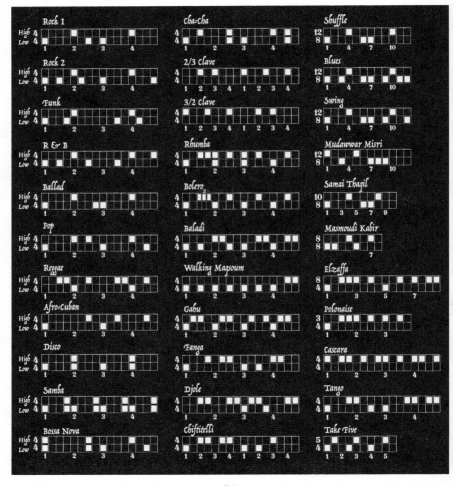

APPENDIX IV - HARMONIES

APPENDIX V - SOLFEGE & MNEMONICS

SOLFEGE/SOLMIZATION

Ut Re Mi Fa Sol La Si Ut
Gamma-Ut = Gamut

Ut queant laxis, Re-sonare fibris, Mi-ra gestorum

Fa-muli tuorom, Sol-ve polluti, La-bii reatum,

Sa-ncte Iohannes

(8TH CENTURY PLAINSONG TO JOHN THE BAPTIST)

In the West, three systems have evolved and are in use today:

Fixed Do:
Do Re Mi Fa So La Si Do
Advantages: good for those with perfect pitch,
absolute scale names
Disadvantages: any syllable can have up to 5 sounds
(bb, b, nat, #, x)
seven different key syllabifications

Movable Do, chromatic syllables:
Do Di Re Ri Mi Fa Fi So Si La Li Ti Do ASCENDING
Do Ti Te La Le So Se Fa Mi Me Re Ra Do DESCENDING
Advantages: Illustrates tonic-dominant Do-So
relationships clearly through major and parallel minor,
one syllabification for all scales
Disadvantages: Obscures relative minor relationship, breaks
down with chromatic passages; i.e. no aug3, no dim4

Movable Do, La minor, chromatic syllables:
MAJOR:
Do Di Re Ri Mi Fa Fi So Si La Li Ti Do ASCENDING
Do Ti Te La Le So Se Fa Mi Me Re Ra Do DESCENDING
MINOR:
La Li Ti Do Di Re Ri Mi Fa Fi So Si La ASCENDING
La Le So Se Fa Mi Me Re Ra Do Ti La DESCENDING
Advantages: Reveals the modal and historical
relativity of major and minor
Disadvantages: Masks tonic-dominant Do-So relationship,
breaks down in minor chromatic passages; i.e. no aug5, dim3,
seven different mode syllabifications

MNEMONICS

For Thirds:

TREBLE CLEF, LINES:
Every Good Boy Does Fine
Every Good Boy Deserves Fudge
Elephants Got Big Dirty Feet
Empty Garbage Before Dad Flips

TREBLE CLEF, SPACES:
F-A-C-E, Fun Always Comes Easy

BASS CLEF, LINES:
Great Big Dandelions Fly Away
Good Boys Do Fine Always
Good Boys Deserve Fudge Always
Great Big Deer from Alaska
Great Big Dogs from America
Granny's Boots Don't Fit Aunty

BASS CLEF, SPACES:
All Cars Eat Gas
All Cows Eat Grass
All Children Eat Gum

for Fifths and Fourths:

Give Dorothy An Easter Basket For Christmas
For Christmas Give Dorothy An Easter Basket
Flying Birds Enjoy A Delightful Green Countryside
Birds Enjoy A Delightful Green Countryside Flying

Above: A dodecahedral mapping of the twelve notes of the scale which preserves the tritone oppositions shown in the circle of fifths.